Kandra's Keys:

The Shortest Book on How

to Write Your Book

By

Kandra Albury

Kandra's Keys: The Shortest Book on How to Write Your Book

Copyright © 2018 by Kandra Albury

ISBN: 978-0-9994400-5-6

All rights reserved. No part of this publication may be reproduced, stored in a retrieval system or transmitted in any form or by any means- electronic, mechanical, photocopy, record or any other except for brief quotations in printed reviews, without the permission of the publisher/author.

Printed in the United States of America.

"It's not about how much you say, but what you say."

~Kandra C. Albury

Introduction

Before diving into this book, make a commitment – right now; schedule eight to ten hours per week to work on your manuscript and overall project. There are several moving components that must merge together when authoring a book. So, when "writer's block" occurs [and undoubtedly it will], simply move on to another chapter and or work on another component of your book...

Initially, when I contemplated becoming an author, I retorted typical excuses: "I don't have time!" "I'm not creative or imaginative enough…" My list of excuses played nonstop in my head. Fortunately, I developed a serious zeal about my authorship reality. I quickly realized that it is not a matter of having time; but it is a matter of *scheduling* time, and refusing to cancel, neglect, or postpone authoring appointments. Confirm writing as a hot date with your journal, pen, computer and/or electronic device [I had to learn what times worked best (for me)]. This is like scheduling any other appointment such as a doctor's appointment or dentist appointment – reserve a time that works best with your schedule. I scheduled my *dates* with *"authorship reality"* when my hubby is working on one of his projects and our son has slept into dreamland. During these moments of quietness, I freely steal away… I am peacefully solace with myself, my thoughts, and my creative juices. The melodic flow of classical music serenades me into *my zone*! I feel endowed with an indescribable power that causes me to write truthfully, courageously, and passionately. Every emotion that I can possibly feel is ignited as my fingers glide along the keyboard.

  Becoming an author requires discipline; especially with life's demands of family, careers, hobbies, volunteering in your community, and commitments to church or civic organizations [talk about being stretched super-thin]. Let's not discuss the pressing need to be connected via social media due to *"fear of missing out"* (FOMO). However, when you aspire to become an author, every minute set aside is well-worth it; because you're not just writing a book! You are documenting your legacy (while making it invaluable), affirming your truth, being boldly transparent, and inspiring others with your knowledge/experience... be it personal, professional, or both. Consequently, you must reserve the time weekly, to write and prepare to embark on your literary journey because *your* time *is* **<u>NOW</u>**!

<u>Before continuing, consider the following questions:</u>

1. What are the primary goal(s) for your book?
    a. To reach and educate a certain niche
    b. To accomplish a personal/professional goal
    c. To add to your credentials
    d. To become a bestselling author – think BIG!
    e. To inspire/ motivate others
2. Who will be inspired by my book? / Who will my work speak to?
3. What issue/problem will I address and/or solve?
4. What should the price of my book be?

5. Will I self-publish or use a traditional publisher?
6. Will my book be available as an E-book, hardcover, paperback or in all three formats?
7. What's the vision for the cover?
8. Who should help me with my book? Who will be my cheerleaders?
9. Will I need an illustrator, photographer, and/or a media kit?
10. What is the total cost to write and publish a book?

To answer that question upfront, it will cost you between $2500 - $5000. A breakdown is provided in a later chapter. Don't be alarmed by this amount because most contributors within publishing offer payment options. So, breathe!

If you were unsure of how to answer any of these questions, don't worry the answers are found within this book. Let's get started!

Aspiring Authors' Daily Affirmation Key

Read it.

Speak it.

Write it.

"I have a story to tell and I'm going to tell it–NOW!"

_____

_____

_____

_____

_____

_____

Table of Contents

Kandra's Keys

Key	page
No. 1 Gather the Pieces	1
No. 2 The Start-up Kit	5
No. 3 Set a Completion Date	8
No. 4 Know Your Target	12
No. 5 The Cover	18
No. 6 A Brow-raising Title	27
No. 7 Your Online Presence	30
No. 8 The First Five Chapters	36
No. 9 Pay It Foreword	43
No. 10 The Introduction	46
No. 11 Sock It to 'Em	49
No. 12 Make a Sandwich	55

(Kandra's Key's continued)

<u>Key</u> <u>page</u>

No. 13 **Conquering Writer's Block** 59

No. 14 **Why You Should Self-publish** 62

Master Key
The Good, the Bad, and the Truth 67

Key No. 1

<u>Gather the Pieces</u>

Your journey as an aspiring author has several transitional pieces; don't be intimidated by the process! I will hash-out the details. I commend your courage to tell your story <u>*now*</u>, it has been on hold long enough!

As you write your book, keep the following steps in mind:

1. Schedule a professional photo shoot. This should be booked 45 days after starting your manuscript.

    a. Hire a makeup artist and a stylist to help you look and feel your absolute best!

2. Hire a graphic designer for your cover and marketing materials.

    a. Have your cover designed **<u>first</u>**, so you can promote it immediately.

3. Secure your ISBN. You will need an ISBN for each format (e-Book, paperback, hard cover). An ISBN is $125 and the bar code is $25.

4. Once you've secured your ISBN and you're confident with your title, file for your copyright, online ($35 registration fee), with the Library of Congress that is based in Washington, DC. https://eco.copyright.gov

5. If you self-publish, keep in mind that you cut out the middle-man and you receive all your royalties. There are countless self-publishing companies: Create Space and Ingram Spark are quite popular. There is a set-up fee to begin, $49 for a traditional book and $25 for an e-Book.

6. Release your book cover at least 60 days after you start writing your manuscript. This will allow you to promote your work. It will also provide time to

schedule your book release celebration which includes:

a. Secure a venue (libraries have space at no-cost)/ schedule a two-hour window for the event.

b. Compile a guest list and send invitations.

c. Decide how the celebration will flow (meet and greet or something more formal). You may also want to include guest readers; or share some of your favorite excerpts followed by a Q&A session.

7. You may also consider hosting a virtual release celebration via Facebook live or Instagram live.

8. Create a press release and/or media advisory to invite local media.

9. If you don't know where to start with your manuscript, I highly recommend hiring a literary coach, who can help you hash out the title of your book, chapter titles, talking points/takeaways

for each chapter, and hold you accountable with weekly assignments and coaching calls.

10. Have a website designed or you can design one yourself using Wix.com or you can contract a freelance web designer on Fiver. Ensure all web and book content is thoroughly edited. If you cannot afford a website, create a social media page and use it until you are able to expand your platform for meeting the masses.

Enjoy the journey!

Key No. 2

The Start-up Kit

A carpenter never shows up to build a house without tools and an artist never starts painting without brushes and a canvas. The same principle applies when writing your book. Below is a list of items you need prior to starting your manuscript:

- **Desktop computer or electronic tablet.** This will allow you to compose your manuscript using Microsoft Word or Notepad.

- **Journal and/or digital device (Smart Phone, iPad, laptop or computer).** Use this journal specifically for your literary work. Keep it handy for the times you feel inspired to write beyond your scheduled writing appointments.

- **USB drive** – Label it with your name and phone number. When working on your manuscript - save, save, save [throughout the writing process]. This is a life-saver (literally), especially in the event of a power surge.

- **Email account** – This will allow you to email your document to yourself, in addition to saving it to a USB. Having an email address allows you to quickly share documents and other information with your literary coach or others involved in the process of writing your book. Email accounts are free, easily-accessible, and convenient; and there are several hosts to choose from (Google, Hotmail, Microsoft, and Yahoo).

- **Social media channel** - There are several social media channels available, utilize the one that works best for you and your target audience. Facebook, Twitter, Instagram, and Snapchat are the most viable. You want to create buzz and start positioning yourself as a leading authority *before* you release your book. Do ***NOT*** be afraid to share your truth. It's yours; it *cannot be minimized*.

Share inspirational quotes using various free text on pictures/canvas apps such as Text SWAG or Text Gram.

- **Most importantly, you need support.** Have someone who believes in you and encourages you along your literary journey. Whether it be a spouse, a close friend, or a literary coach such as myself. A literary coach walks aspiring authors through the book-writing process by assigning homework, reviewing assignments, meet manuscript deadlines and by helping them confidently evolve into an author and authority. Literary coaches are experts as it relates to effective storytelling and authorship.

Key No. 3

<u>Set a Completion Deadline</u>

Your investment in *this* book, proves you are ready to tell your story **<u>*now*</u>**. Thus, keep the following information in mind. Envision your completed project, and set your manuscript completion date **<u>*now*</u>**! Go ahead, pull out your cell phone or calendar and take care of this first. Writing your story should take approximately 90 days to complete, contingent upon your life's demands. As a literary coach, I typically work with clients up to 120 days - total. However, if the client is serious but needs an additional month, I will continue our collaboration. Let's assess your seriousness. Fill in the completion date below. Now, take out your cellphone and set reminders on your calendar. Then put a written reminder on your bathroom mirror. This date does not insinuate that the editing of your book will be completed; but the writing will be finished. You will hire an editor to polish, enhance, and "perfect" your manuscript. Go on, set that date – right now!

I will complete my manuscript by
_____.

Before your book is completed, start promoting it at least 60 days pre-completion, to create buzz and pre-orders through your website. Yes, I said *your* website. We will discuss this in a later chapter.

Now that you have established a completion date, you **must** commit to is writing at least 8 to 10 hours per week.

I will dedicate _____ hours per week, to meet my writing deadline.

Begin with five hours of writing per week and build your tenacity. If you can commit to more than 8-10 hours per week, do it! Nothing compares to the feeling of meeting a goal early.

Before you start writing, format a template in Microsoft Word in the following order. Position these titles at the top of the page in the order below:

- Title page
- Copyright page
- Acknowledgements
- Table of contents
- Foreword
- Preface
- Introduction
- Table of Contents

Put the headings on separate pages by holding the control key (lower left on your computer keyboard) and pressing enter (at the same time). Always save as you go, by saving the document as the title of the book or the initials of the book including the completion date. For example, my book "From Food Stamps to Favor," looked like this - FFSTF_8_20_15. Every time you stop working on the document, save it and email it to yourself. Also save it to your USB drive. You can also use Dropbox or Cloud. Always save, save, s-a-v-e!

Key No. 4

Know Your Target

Take a moment, and ask yourself what kind of book you desire to write? Will it be fiction or non-fiction? Will it be your memoir, a motivational text, or inspirational guide? Who is your target audience? Will it be marketed towards children, teens, women, men, or both? Is your book for Christians, mainstream audiences, or both sectors? Is it for those who are married, single, separated, or divorced? Take a few seconds to brainstorm these questions.

Space is provided below to help you pinpoint your target audience:

Type of book:

Target audience:

What's the problem?

Now that you've identified your target audience, it's time to think about the premise of your message; or, should I say, the primary focus of your literary work? At this point, picture yourself as a scientist conducting an experiment. Before a scientist begins any experiment, a hypothesis is established, which is an educated guess about a problem. The question remains at the forefront of their minds as the experiment is conducted. While writing your book, I want you to identify a problem that your book will solve or the issue you've decided to address. In answering the problem or confronting the issue, you are positioning yourself to become an expert or leading authority/voice. My professional advice, to you, is to prepare now and become comfortable with being an expert as well as being interviewed. You may not refer to yourself as an expert, but I am confident there is something you do in a matter of minutes or hours that takes other people days or even weeks. Besides, life experiences train us to be novice experts, whether we have an official title, credentials, or none. The more you apply and build your skill set, the more you can speak as an expert. Take for instance, my husband; he makes the best peanut butter and jelly sandwiches ever! He can tell you which is better for spreading – jelly or jam and the best brand to use. He can also tell you whether Wonder bread is better than Merita for making PB&J sandwiches. Lastly, he will tell you if using a butter knife or spoon works better for creating America's all-time favorite sandwich. Say it with me, "I am an expert! "

After I published the signature book in the Feisty Four Children's Book Series, "Don't You Dare Touch Me There," I appeared on various news stations and did cameos for an array of community events. Suddenly, I was being introduced as a "Sexual Abuse Prevention Expert!" The first time it happened, I was slightly intimidated because I didn't know all that I needed to know to be an authority, but I knew enough to talk about prevention from my own vantage point as a conqueror of childhood sexual abuse. I stood in my truth, but that wasn't enough. I needed to learn statistical data and how to apply it to my book as well as broader subject matter. To overcome the intimidation, I expanded my knowledge about sexual abuse to position myself as the best sexual abuse prevention expert and children's advocate known to the literary world and beyond.

    I participated in a sexual abuse prevention training offered by the organization known as Darkness to Light. I drove about three hours from Gainesville, FL. to Polk County, FL., for a two-hour Stewards of Children training; the training was $25. Following the enlightening session, I spoke with the facilitator and asked what I needed to do to become a facilitator to offer the trainings in my community and surrounding areas. A year later, I became a certified Darkness to

Light Stewards of Children Sexual Abuse Prevention Training facilitator. This allowed me to offer the two-hour trainings to everyday community members, as well as to youth-serving organizations in my area. The training armed me with statistical data about childhood sexual abuse that I wasn't aware of by simply being an author. Today, when I speak to adults as a sexual abuse prevention authority and a children's advocate, I possess information on the subject matter coupled with a great prevention resource for parents – my book. Again, embrace becoming and being an expert!

Key No. 5

The Cover

You have a mere thirty-second window to make an impression that moves someone from the role of a spectator to an investor. Your book *must* have visual appeal, there's no way around it… we live in a visual society. Potential customers scan the cover, first. So, hiring a professional graphic designer to work their magic is mandatory for all book cover designs as well as promotional materials, which should be properly branded using the same colors, fonts, and style. Professionally trained graphic designers make sure your best work is front and center in the marketplace. For this project, make the investment and hire a professional graphic designer. Their fee may range between $250-$500 for a book cover design. Make sure if you are going to have a traditional book as well as an e-Book you will need the graphic designer to design just a front cover for the electronic version of your book. Sometimes the price may depend on what's involved in the scope of work. Additionally, I highly recommend that you have professional photoshoot. So, whether you are using your photo(s) on the front cover or the back cover, it will cost between $150-$300 per hour; the photographer will include high resolution photos as a part of the purchase package. Be sure to request high resolution, digital photos because you don't want your picture (whether on the front or back of your book) to appear blurry or pixilated. You want everything about you and your finished product to be professional, and worthy of respect within the marketplace.

Visual appeal is a key selling point. Keep your title under ten words. This keeps the cover clean and clutter free. A good title should strike a chord with readers. Something about *your* title should resonate with them! Most importantly, it should be short, simple, and sensational. When you have established a title for your book, Google it to make sure there isn't a book published with the same title. You don't want to receive a "cease and desist" letter from a legal representative because your title matches another title, or is a word or two off from someone else's book that is published with a copyright.

Another selling point is your table of contents. Use short phrases and avoid using complete sentences to name chapters. The table of contents tells a story as well. Use chapter titles to intrigue, entertain, and maximize the reader's curiosity. You want readers do a double-take when they see your book whether you unveil the cover online or at a special event. Keep in mind, several [major] online retailers usually share the cover, the first few pages of your book's interior, as well as the back cover. Consequently, everything must be well-written and edited from cover-to-cover.

The size and finish of your book must also be considered. I recommend looking at what's on *your* bookshelf, visiting a local bookstore, and/or library to help you determine the size and the finish of your book. Books can have a shiny finish, a matte finish, soft back, or enclosed in a case laminate hard back. Therefore, when [and if] you face writer's block…there's always another component of your project to work on until *your* writer's block passes.

Photo Shoot Ready

Schedule your photo shoot for the cover as soon as you begin working on your manuscript. As you are writing your book, think about what you would like the cover to look like; and then share this information with your publisher or literary coach. While there are many steps involved when writing a book, completing the cover is your priority. You'll be surprised how focused and disciplined you become after you see your cover in its completed format. It's just like a mom holding a newborn baby for the first time. Once the cover is finished, share a "coming soon" post or "coming spring of 20__". Have your designer put a professional announcement together and share it. Completing the cover within the first two-three months of working on your book, provides time to find a professional photographer to schedule your photo shoot, a makeup artist to enhance your look, a stylist to dress you for the session, as well as a professional graphic designer to complete the look for the cover.

    If you will be working with a publisher or self-publishing agent, they may include these services in their contract; if not, simply ask for a recommendation. Trust me, how you look, and the finished product is a direct reflection of them and the work they do to guide their clients through the process. If you plan to lose a little weight prior to your photo shoot, this can be accomplished this within 30-60 days if you consistently eat healthy and exercise. Completion of the cover will build excitement and help you create buzz about your book prior to it being released. I recommend that you release your book on a special day; it can be your birthday or another special date. Timing is everything. Whether you choose to put your photo on the front cover or on the back cover of your book, hire a professional stylist to help you take your look to the next level! Whatever color you use, incorporate it into your promotional materials to strengthen *your* brand's identity. Have fun with your photo shoot and have the photographer play music or take your own portable speaker. Include your favorite color in the attire you wear during the shoot and integrate it into your logo (if you feel the need to have one). A professionally trained stylist such as, *The* Cathy Norman, CEO of *Intuitive Designs and Fashion Consulting (IDFC)* in

Gainesville, Florida; IDFC works with clients to not only achieve a new look but their best look for their own unique body type with an extra flare and sizzle. I also recommend at least two-three outfit changes assembled by your stylist with your input, of course.

Again, promote your book using your professionally designed and captivating cover at least 60 days prior to the book's distribution. During this time, accept pre-orders via your website –Yes, I said website *again*! We will talk about this key shortly.

Aspiring Authors' Daily Affirmation Key

Read it.

Speak it.

Write it.

"I am creative, passionate, and I have something to say."

_____

_____

_____

_____

_____

Key No. 6

A Brow-Raising Title

When thinking about your title, be sure to add color, punch, and creativity. Play on words but don't confuse the reader. Add a twist of suspense and leave the potential reader curious enough to purchase your book. Don't forget to Google search your title to ensure your title does not provoke unwanted legal attention. Your title, including the subtitle, should be no more than 10 words and have a resonating dynamism.

Your title is the second punch of dynamism to meet the eyes of your readers (the first punch is your cover). The title *cannot be* overly wordy, and it must have that "eyebrow-raising" factor. The final blow is the table of contents, and it must knock them off their feet. When titling your chapters, be creative and use short bursts to deliver the final punch. Readers will scan the table of content to determine if the book is worth the investment. Allow your table of contents to pique readers' interest and guarantee the sale. Thirty-seconds is all you get to present and sell your story, make the most of it!

Below is a warm up exercise. Google search the name of US Olympian and Gold Medalist, Gabby Douglas. Read a couple of articles about her. Come up with a book title, create eyebrow-raising titles for chapters 1-3 of her book, and articulate a vision for the cover. At the end of this assignment, I will reveal what I came up with, as well as the creative responses of some workshop participants for this warm up activity.

Book Titles:

Chapter titles:

Suggested Titles:
- I'm Not My Flipping Hair
- Kinky Hair, Shiny Medals…The Road to the Gold
- My Golden Ponytail

Now that you're warmed up, you should be ready to hash-out some potential book titles below:

_____
_____
_____
_____
_____
_____
_____

Key No. 7

Your Online Presence

A website solidifies your global presence and allows you to do business from anywhere in the world. Your website should be visually-appealing, easy to navigate, properly branded, and all the content should be thoroughly edited and include the following tabs:

- **About** - Your biographical information is outlined here, along with a professional head shot taken by your photographer. The photos from your photo shoot should be utilized as much as possible. Include information about where you were born, currently reside (you can use just the state), marital status, children, profession/professional experience, education, and hobbies. Don't forget to include your personal mantra/life motto.

- **Services** - Serious authors evolve into experts/leading authorities, inspirational or motivational speakers. Some offer read-alouds, roundtable discussions, focus groups, and/or consulting services.

- **Store** - It is important to sell your book as well as other promotional products via your website. Most sites have a widget that allow you to incorporate a shopping cart as well as add tax for your state. Be sure to use images of the products as well as a simple description.

- **Contact** - When a potential client/customer wants to reach out to you, be sure to have your contact information readily available. This can be an email form that is completed and opened from your email account. Some people use a separate business line, which is a tax deduction.

- **Keep in touch** - This allows you to collect email addresses of those who visit your website. It also gives you an opportunity to send out a newsletter with promotional specials or share your latest blog posts directly with your followers.

Expect to spend between $800 - $1,000 (possibly more) on a professionally designed website. My husband is my web designer, his work is impeccable. You can also use Fiver, which is an app in which freelancers offer their services at a discounted price. Keep in mind that your website is a continuation of your brand.

So, what is a brand? A brand is a name given to a product or service. You are your brand and you cannot separate your name from your work, particularly as an author. Think about McDonald's golden arches. The first thing that comes to my mind are their irresistible French fries. As an author, you will also be known for the work that you do beyond writing your book(s). You may even evolve into an advocate, an inspirational speaker, trainer, workshop facilitator, or consultant. Wherever your literary journey takes you, always be true to your brand. Be professional online as well in as in person. Remain touchable, teachable, and continuously kind. I have learned that having a pleasant attitude, great personality, and upstanding character sells who you are before a book is ever purchased. You are a package deal and all of it contributes to your overall character. Whether you want to be on the internet or not, I can *almost* guarantee if you Google your name and click search - something will pop up [do it now, call my bluff]. Thus, is it imperative to be an integral person! Also, as you evolve into your profession as an author, you must courageously come from the background and dismiss timidity. Reach out to organizations and individuals to share your excitement about your work. *It's your time to shine!*

Notes:

_____

_____

_____

_____

_____

_____

_____

_____

Aspiring Authors' Daily Affirmation Key:

Read it.

Speak it.

Write it.

"I see worth in my story and my story is worth telling."

_____

_____

_____

_____

_____

Key No. 8

The First Five Chapters

The fabulous five are the first five chapters of your book. You may have more than five and if you do, call them the super seven or exciting eight. Whatever you call them, make them fierce, but most importantly, name the chapters dynamically. Keep them simple and to the point. Avoid using complete sentences to name your chapters. Don't forget, your table of contents tells a story and helps to seal the sell. Remember everything about your literary work tells a story before it's ever purchased. Ultimately, your visual and written presentation contributes to the success of your product in the marketplace.

Below space is provided to write down your chapter titles as well as the takeaways for each of them. Takeaways or talking points are key topics that you will discuss in five to seven paragraphs or more. These can be anecdotes (short stories) that provide readers with additional insight; truth and lessons learned from your experiences. This is allows readers to glean from you; thereby adding value to the reader's life. Take time to think about the underlying theme for your book. The underlying theme should inspire readers to think, progress, or both. Once you've jotted down writing points for each chapter, try writing them in order so that your content flows easily and your reader doesn't get lost. Remember, as the conductor of the train; you must ensure you don't lose readers along the journey.

Brainstorm your book titles below:

_____
_____
_____
_____
_____
_____
_____
_____
_____
_____

Chapter 1: Title and three takeaways.
Remember to keep the title under 10 words

_____
_____
_____
_____
_____
_____
_____
_____
_____
_____

Chapter 2: Title and three takeaways.

_____
_____
_____
_____
_____
_____
_____
_____

Chapter 3: Title and three takeaways.

_____
_____
_____
_____
_____
_____
_____
_____
_____

Chapter 4: Title and three takeaways.

_____

_____
_____
_____
_____
_____
_____
_____
_____
_____

Chapter 5: Title and three takeaways.

_____
_____
_____
_____
_____
_____
_____
_____
_____

Things are about to get wonderfully exciting because you're going to share your vision for the cover. Be as descriptive as possible. Do you see yourself on the cover? If not, what do you see? If you see yourself on the cover, what are you wearing?

Keep in mind that while you may have a vision for your cover, less is more and a professionally trained graphic designer can create a final product that will knock your vision out of the park.

Write your vision for the cover.

_____
_____
_____
_____
_____
_____
_____
_____
_____
_____
_____
_____
_____

Aspiring Authors' Daily Affirmation Key:

Read it.

Speak it.

Write it.

"I will write with respect, responsibility, and transparency."

_____

_____

_____

_____

_____

Key No. 9

<u>Pay it Foreword</u>

Decide if your book should have a foreword and if it does, who will write it. The foreword adds to the credibility of your book and is usually written by someone other than yourself. It's an honor to have someone write your foreword. The foreword shouldn't be too long and should speak about you and what makes your work notable. Name a couple of people worthy of writing your foreword, this is a person of integrity and honor. Remember, do not text or email them to request this great privilege. This should be an official phone call or conversation over lunch or dinner. Use the space below to jot down some names of people you will consider for this important task. Think about why they would be a good fit for writing the foreword. In some instances, authors write their own foreword. I did in my memoir, "From Food Stamps to Favor". If you'd like more information on forewords, simply browse the contents of the books that you have on your personal bookshelf.

Notes:

_____

_____

_____

_____

_____

_____

_____

_____

Aspiring Authors' Daily Affirmation Key:

Read it.

Speak it.

Write it.

"My book is my legacy and I am making it invaluable today."

_____

_____

_____

_____

_____

Key No. 10

The Introduction

Your introduction foreshadows your book but does not reveal the entire storyline. The introduction can pick up from a specific chapter in your book. Sometimes the last line in your book can be the opening line of your introduction. Whatever you do, do not give away the entire story in the introduction. It should be well written with flagrant appeal because, again, you're taking your readers on a journey. Consider the introduction as the final boarding call before the train leaves the station. While you – the conductor, may know where you're going, the passengers (your readers) do not. Truthfully, you never know where a reader will start… so, it is best to make sure everything is cohesive and well written, from cover to cover. Set aside two hours to start writing your introduction, but before you get started you need an aspiring author's kit.

Notes:

_____

_____

_____

_____

_____

_____

_____

_____

_____

_____

Aspiring Authors' Daily Affirmation Key:

Read it.

Speak it.

Write it.

"I am committed to making my journey exciting and uplifting."

_____

_____

_____

_____

_____

Key No. 11

<u>Sock It to 'em</u>

Don't forget to sock it to 'em when writing. Write with purpose and vibrancy. A dear friend of mine says "puts sugar in what we say and salt in what we do." It is your responsibility, as an author, to take the reader on a journey. You are the conductor of the train and you are helping readers realize their story in your story. If they can't find their story in yours, then incite emotion: make them feel, make them believe, and make them connect. If you were angry, help them relate to your anger, and if you're happy, cause them to experience your joy. Paint a picture in their minds of where you are in the story. Make sure you're writing your best work simply because you want nothing but your absolute best in the marketplace. In addition, readers will tell others about your book via social media, word of mouth, or on a review website such as an Amazon, Barnes & Noble, or Books-A-Million. Keep this in mind as you tell your story. Use the space below to practice writing some opening sentences to your chapter titles. The opening sentence can be short and to the point or captivating. Be at one with your thoughts. Whatever you do, don't forget to add sugar and salt to your words.

Sometimes in socking it to 'em, you are socking it to yourself. Writing about difficult times in your life isn't easy… you are granting yourself permission to revisit dark places in your life. This is never easy but can be done masterfully and responsibly by writing from a place of wholeness. So even if you're angry, you won't stay in that place of anger. The beauty of writing is that the journey has both highs and lows, which allows the author to share the bitter and the sweet harmoniously. There will be times you will need to take a break from writing, but don't become too relaxed regarding your writing because you don't want to lose your fervor. Lastly, writing about difficult or an extremely personal life experience is not easy, but you want your reader to be empowered, enlightened, and liberated by your truth and transparency. This is the responsibility of the author; because at the end of the book, you want to be a well-respected.

Color Your Words. What will I say that no one else is saying? How can I say it differently? Be unique and courageous, but find harmony. Words are *powerful*, yet they can also be mere ink on paper. Write with color.

Total Value. How will my book add value to the lives of readers? Purpose…

Help readers to find their story in yours. If not, help them to empathize with you and feel your emotions [establish the connection]. Notes:

_____

_____

_____

_____

_____

_____

_____

Notes, continued:

Aspiring Authors' Daily Affirmation Key:

Read it.

Speak it.

Write it.

"It's not how much I say, it's what I say."

_____

_____

_____

_____

_____

Key No. 12

<u>Make a Sandwich</u>

The opening line of your book is equally important as the closing line. Make sure the opening line of the book as well as each chapter captures the attention of your readers. Say what no one else is saying, or say what everyone else is saying but with your own twist of truth, boldness, and shock value are essential. It is OK to say what most people think, but aren't brave enough to say! Remember to be responsible, yet brutally honest.

Consider writing your book like making a sandwich. When you visit *Subway*, the national and international sandwich chain, first thing the sandwich artist asks is what type of sandwich you'd like, followed by the type of bread and cheese you want. Then the meat is added, followed by the cheese and the toppings (lettuce, tomatoes, onion, bell peppers, olives, pickles, and/or banana peppers. After that, the condiments are added…vinegar, oil, salt, pepper, mustard, mayonnaise, and/or dressing… then the sandwich is finished! You are happily content because you have something you'll enjoy for breakfast, lunch, or dinner. Same thing applies when writing a book. You want to produce a product that you will be proud of in the marketplace. With this comes making sure you're not giving the reader fluff. Keep in mind that it's not how much you say, but what you say that matters! Readers know when you're just stringing them along… so, do not waste their time.

In today's world, it is no secret that between family, smart phones, apps, and social media we are competing for the attention of our targeted audience. So, keep your message short, simple, and to the point…while adding value to the life of the reader. Don't forget, your readers will use social media to spread the word about your book –be it positive or negative. Let's hope their feedback is something you will appreciate and/or share as well.

Notes:

_____

_____

_____

_____

Notes, continued:

Key No. 13

<u>Conquering Writer's Block</u>

Countless clients have told me they hit a brick wall. Below are a few simple tips to help you conquer writer's block:

1. Pray/meditate or take a walk.
2. Schedule time to write when it is quiet, and you can focus.
3. Write to classical music.
4. *Refer to your manuscript completion goal reminders.
5. Step away for a few minutes.
6. Write in another chapter or create the back-cover content or content for promo cards (samples are provided at the end of this book).

7. Do not take off more than three days from writing.

8. Stick to your goal of eight to ten hours of writing per week.

9. Write your back-cover content. You may want individuals to provide review quotes about the work for your back-cover. Reach out to them once you've completed chapter one. Have them review it and add a quote. You do not have to send the entire manuscript and if you do, save it with a watermark in Microsoft Word) click on the "Page Layout" tab then click "Watermark" and choose proof. Save what you're sending as a PDF by going to "save as," click on the drop-down arrow that has document name and click "document type" and select PDF.

*Also place reminders in places that you check frequently, such as a bathroom mirror, the inside door of the medicine cabinet, the back of your front door, above the key holder, or on your speedometer. If you don't want people to know what you're doing, call it "My big day". If someone asks and you're not ready to share, simply tell them, it is for a personal goal you're working towards.

Key No. 14

<u>Why You Should Self-Publish</u>

To write and publish your book, it will cost you between $3500 and $5000, depending on the route you take. I am a huge proponent of self-publishing. If you choose to self-publish, you automatically cut out the middle men (the publisher as well as the printer). All your royalties are paid directly to you, which is the first benefit of self-publishing your own book; you get paid first! The word, self-publish is an intimidating word but when you hire a literary agent or consultant, they will walk you through the process and ensure that everything goes smoothly for you.

Here's the breakdown of the $3500 - $5000 cost:

- Illustrator/Graphic designer (for cover and promo materials): $500- $800

- Photo shoot for cover and promo materials: $150-$250

- Marketing/promotional packages typically include:

    - Book cover

    - Business cards

    - Social media custom cover design

    - Promo cards (to include life quotes, product and head shot w/ website and social media handles). Also "coming soon" announcing book release

    - Pull up banner

    - Social media cover photo

- Stylist to customize your look for your photo shoot. Their fee for shopping excursions will start at $75 per hour.

You will need to set a budget for your ensemble that you will wear for your photo shoot.

- ISBNs are $125 each and you need one for each format for your book.

- A bar code is $25 and you only need one for your book not the E-book.

- The set-up fee for the book is $50 and $25 for the E-book.

- E-book conversion is $.60 per page.

- A literary/writing coach fee may start at $950 and go up to the thousands. This person coaches you through the writing process and makes sure your manuscript flows smoothly. A coach asks the tough questions. Coaches know the inner workings of the process and will thoroughly guide you through the process, which includes formatting of the manuscript for submission and confirming distribution. However, distribution incurs a separate fee, and can start at $950.

- Some editors charge $10 per page or by the word. Some even charge by the hour.

- Website costs start at $850 (and increase based on the need of the client).

Aspiring Authors' Daily Affirmation Key:

Read it.

Speak it.

Write it.

"Writing is liberating–Let's get free together!"

_____

_____

_____

_____

_____

Master Key

<u>The Good, the Bad, and the Truth</u>

As an aspiring author, don't expect to make lots of money right away, but remain consistent and strategic. Focus on your passion and purpose for doing the work. Find ways to network with others by researching local interest groups or conferences for authors, editors, and mentors. You'll be amazed by the number of aspiring authors who are also starting their literary journey.

In closing, I want to leave you with the master key (a quick review) of some of the previously mentioned information that can be used as a handy checklist:

1. Decide upfront if you will need a writing/publishing consulting. They will hold you accountable and make sure you meet your manuscript completion deadline. They will also walk you through the publishing and distribution process.

2. Set your manuscript completion deadline for three to five months out. Try not to exceed six months.

3. Write with truth, conviction, and transparency

4. Have fun! This is such an exciting time. If you happen to encounter writer's block, write your abbreviated bio and book synopsis for your back cover. Try not to exceed three-five paragraphs. Your bio should highlight your marital status, education, profession, hobbies/interests, and children/pets. You can also work in another chapter, or work on quotes to go in between chapters as well as your promotional cards.

5. Decide if your book will have a foreword and reach out to the person you want to write it. Do the same for testimonials/endorsements for your back cover.

6. Schedule eight-ten hours of writing per week.

7. Purchase your ISBNs as soon as you know the title of your book. Keep in mind that you will need an ISBN for each format (paperback, hard cover, e-Book). An ISBN costs $125 and a barcode is $25. You will not need a barcode for an e-Book.

8. Research stylists (to dress you for your photo shoot), makeup artists, photographers, and graphic designers to begin packaging your product and shaping your brand identity.

9. Schedule your photo shoot and have an assistant accompany you.

10. Decide on the size, finish, and price of your book.

11. Start planning your book signing.

Your brand and visual representation in the marketplace are key, which is why I stress the importance of investing in a professional graphic designer. The fliers below were created for various community events. They are often included in school district's newsletters or on community boards.

The following graphics are promo cards that I have used on social media sites such as Facebook, Instagram, and Twitter. They are great for shaping your brand and message.

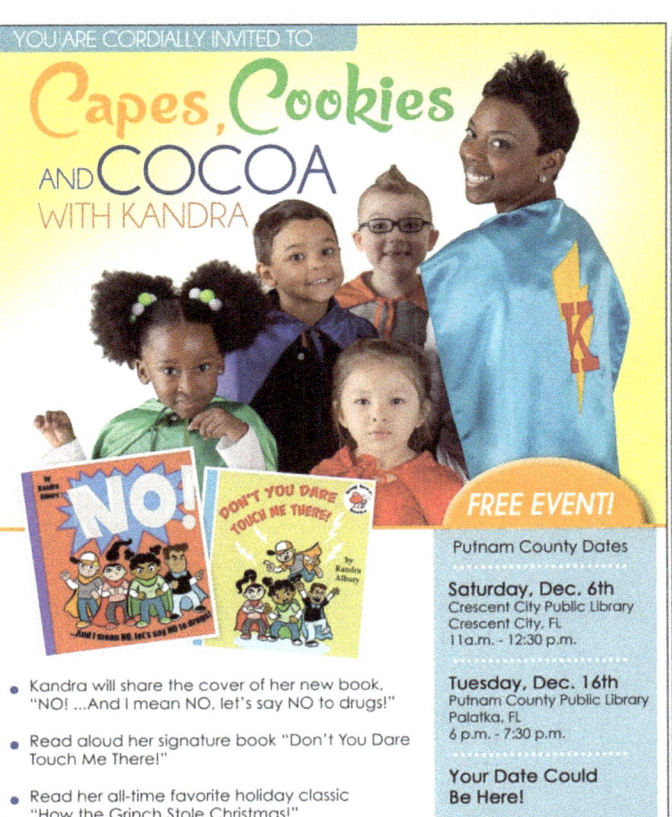

Marketing/promotional materials are essential. Be sure to include the following items:

- **Business cards** (front and back is optional). Include: Name, title, email, website and phone number. Don't forget to invest in a business card holder to keep them clean and neat.

- **Promotional card** (your head shot/product shot) with website and social media handles. Use a promotional card to announce your book release. Use a phrase such as: "Coming Summer 2018."

- **Pull up banner**.

- **Media kit** that will include: Professional head shot, bio, product sheet w/ services you provide, and a Q&A form. This should be saved as a PDF and should be downloadable from your website.

The cover of my memoir: Created by a professional graphic designer.

I invested $750 to have each book in the Feisty Four Children's Book Series illustrated. The picture books are between 33-38 pages. Total investment: $2,250. Most service providers for publishing offer payment plans in which the client pays 50 percent down and pays the balance in installments.

Professional head shots

Professional head shots are a must. I recommend updating them every three to five years. However, if your appearance drastically changes, have them taken sooner.

Follow me on social media and join the Aspiring Author's Ink. Facebook group.

www.ingramcontent.com/pod-product-compliance
Lightning Source LLC
Chambersburg PA
CBHW051602010526
44118CB00023B/2790